Why Great Companies Miss the Next Big Thing.

By Carol Sichembo.

Introduction: The Innovation Graveyard

- Introduce the concept of the "Innovation Blind Spot" and its prevalence in successful companies.
- Explore case studies of companies that missed major innovations, like Nokia and Kodak.
- Highlight the importance of recognizing and overcoming blind spots for continued success.
- **Chapter 1: Success Can Be Blinding:** How past achievements can create a resistance to change.
- **Chapter 2: The Cult of the Status Quo:** Exploring the tendency to favor existing processes and business models.
- **Chapter 3: Fear of Failure and the Innovation Paradox:** How risk aversion can stifle creativity and innovation.
- **Chapter 4: Silencing Dissent: The Peril of Groupthink in Decision-Making** The importance of diverse perspectives and challenging assumptions.
- **Chapter 5: Cultivating a Culture of Innovation:** Strategies to foster creativity and embrace new ideas.
- **Chapter 6: Embracing Disruption:** How to see disruption not as a threat but as an opportunity.
- **Chapter 7: Building Bridges Between Departments:** Encouraging collaboration and information sharing across different functions.

- **Chapter 8: The Power of Customer Insights:** How understanding customer needs can drive innovation.
- **Chapter 9: Learning from the Mavericks**: **Analyzing companies known for innovative success.
- **Chapter 10: Future-Focused Thinking:** **Developing strategies to scan the horizon for emerging trends.
- **Chapter 11: Building an Innovation Engine:** Creating a dedicated system for identifying and testing new ideas.
- **Chapter 12: Leading for Innovation:** **The role of leadership in fostering a culture of innovation and change.

Conclusion:

Introduction: The Innovation Graveyard

The gleaming Silicon Valley office hummed with a frenetic energy. Beanbag chairs adorned the open floor plan, motivational posters plastered the walls, and a ping-pong table sat in the corner, a testament to the company's commitment to a "cool" work culture. Yet, a sense of unease lingered beneath the surface. Sales figures were stagnating, the once-revolutionary product line was beginning to feel stale, and a gnawing fear pulsated through the veins of the company – the fear of becoming another relic in the ever-expanding graveyard of innovation.

This company, once a pioneer in its industry, had fallen victim to a silent killer – the **Innovation Blind Spot**. Defined as the tendency of successful companies to miss out on the next big thing, this blind spot is a pervasive phenomenon that has claimed countless victims, from industry giants like Kodak and Blockbuster to seemingly nimble startups.

We've all witnessed the cautionary tales. Kodak, the undisputed leader in film photography, failed to anticipate the digital revolution, clinging to its outdated technology until it was too late. Blockbuster, the undisputed king of video rentals, scoffed at the upstart Netflix, dismissing the concept of online streaming as a passing fad. These are just a few of the countless companies that have been blindsided by innovation, their dominance crumbling to dust as they clung desperately to the past.

But what exactly is this innovation blind spot? Why does it ensnare even the most successful companies? The answer lies in a complex interplay of factors. Success itself can be a breeding ground for complacency. Companies that have achieved market leadership often struggle to maintain the same level of innovation that propelled them to the top. Past victories lull them into a false sense of security, fostering a belief that their current model is infallible.

This complacency breeds a culture of **status quo bias**, a preference for the familiar over the unknown. Processes, procedures, and business models that once fueled success become sacred cows, immune to questioning or change. The very systems that propelled a company to the top can become shackles that bind it to the past, hindering its ability to adapt to a rapidly evolving market landscape.

Furthermore, the fear of failure can act as a powerful deterrent to innovation. Companies become risk-averse, prioritizing short-term gains over long-term bets on unproven ideas. This risk aversion stifles creativity, creating an environment where innovative ideas are met with skepticism and hesitation. This "innovation paradox" exists — a company needs to embrace risk to stay ahead, but fear of failure can paralyze them from taking the necessary risks.

Perhaps the most insidious aspect of the innovation blind spot is the phenomenon of **groupthink**. In a culture where conformity and agreement are valued, dissenting voices are often silenced. Employees hesitate to challenge the status quo or propose disruptive ideas for fear of being ostracized or ignored. This leads to a myopic vision, where the entire company becomes blind to emerging trends and potential threats from outside disruptors.

The consequences of the innovation blind spot are dire. Companies that fail to adapt find themselves left behind, their market share shrinking as nimbler competitors seize the opportunities they missed. Employees become disillusioned, innovation stalls, and the once-dynamic company descends into a state of mediocrity, ultimately facing the harsh reality of the marketplace.

But here's the good news: the innovation blind spot is not an inevitable fate. There is a path forward, a way for companies to break free from the shackles of the past and embrace the future. This book will serve as your guide on this journey. Over the next few chapters, we'll delve into the anatomy of the innovation blind spot, exploring the psychological and organizational factors that contribute to its development. We'll then equip you with the tools and strategies to overcome this blind spot, fostering a culture of innovation that will keep your company at the forefront of change.

By the time you turn the final page, you'll be armed with a comprehensive understanding of the innovation blind spot and the powerful tools needed to avoid its pitfalls. You'll learn how to cultivate a culture of creativity, embrace disruption, and build a robust system for identifying and seizing the next big thing. This book is not a eulogy for innovation, but a clarion call to action – a call to break free from the past and embrace the boundless potential of the future.

The innovation graveyard is littered with cautionary tales, but it doesn't have to be your company's future. Join us on this journey, and together, we'll ensure your company thrives in the face of disruption and emerges as a champion of innovation.

- **Chapter 1: Success Can Be Blinding:** How past achievements can create a resistance to change.

The weight of past victories can be a double-edged sword for any company. While a history of success brings undeniable benefits, it can also cultivate a dangerous complacency, a resistance to change that can ultimately lead to stagnation and decline. This chapter explores how the very achievements that propel a company to the top can become a blind spot, hindering its ability to adapt to an ever-evolving marketplace.

The Success Trap: Case Studies of Companies Blinded by Glory

1. Kodak (Film Photography): For decades, Kodak reigned supreme in the film photography industry. Their iconic yellow box and innovative film technology made them a household name. However, Kodak failed to anticipate the digital revolution, clinging to their tried-and-true film technology as the market shifted towards digital cameras. By the time they entered the digital market, they were far behind nimbler competitors, ultimately filing for bankruptcy in 2012.

2. Blockbuster (Video Rental): Blockbuster dominated the video rental industry, offering a vast selection of movies and a convenient brick-and-mortar experience. However, they scoffed at the nascent online streaming service Netflix, dismissing it as a niche market. This resistance to adapt to a changing consumer landscape, where convenience and online access were becoming increasingly important, led to Blockbuster's decline and eventual bankruptcy in 2010.

3. Sears (Department Stores): Once a retail giant, Sears was known for its wide selection of merchandise and dependable customer service. However, they failed to adapt to the rise of online shopping and discount retailers. Their reliance on outdated business models and slow response to the changing retail landscape led to a steady decline in market share, culminating in bankruptcy filings in 2018.

4. Research In Motion (BlackBerry): For a period, BlackBerry smartphones were ubiquitous in the business world, renowned for their secure messaging and productivity features. However, they underestimated the rise of touchscreens and user-friendly interfaces, clinging to their physical keyboards as the market shifted towards iPhones and Android devices. This resistance to adapt this led to a rapid decline in market share and ultimately, the company's sidelining in the mobile phone industry.

5. My Space (Social Media): MySpace was once the undisputed king of social media, boasting millions of users and a vibrant online community. However, they failed to keep pace with the evolving social media landscape, clinging to their original design and functionalities while competitors like Facebook offered a more dynamic and user-friendly experience. MySpace's inability to adapt led to a mass exodus of users and its gradual decline in the social media sphere.

6. Borders (Bookstores): Borders was a major player in the bookstore industry, offering a vast selection of books and a comfortable browsing experience. However, they failed to recognize the threat posed by online retailers like Amazon, neglecting to invest in a strong online presence. Their reliance on brick-and-mortar stores in a market increasingly dominated by online shopping led to financial difficulties and eventual bankruptcy in 2011.

These companies are just a few examples of how past success can create a resistance to change. The comfort zone of past victories can blind companies to emerging trends and the need to adapt their business models. It's crucial to remember that success is not a permanent state.

Chapter 2: The Cult of the Status Quo: Where Yesterday's Success Stifles Tomorrow's Innovation

The inertia of success can be a powerful force. In Chapter 1, we explored how past achievements can create a resistance to change, a phenomenon we termed the "Success Blind Spot." This chapter delves deeper, examining the concept of the "Cult of the Status Quo" – the tendency of successful companies to become overly comfortable with existing processes and business models, hindering their ability to innovate and adapt in a dynamic marketplace.

Comfort Over Change: The Allure of the Status Quo

Companies that achieve market dominance often develop a deep-seated belief in the superiority of their existing ways of doing business. Processes become ingrained, hierarchies solidified, and business models viewed as sacrosanct. This comfort zone fosters a culture that prioritizes stability and efficiency over innovation and disruption.

The Case of Nokia:

Nokia's fall from grace in the mobile phone industry serves as a cautionary tale of the dangers of clinging to the status quo. Nokia dominated the market for years, renowned for its sturdy and reliable phones. Their Symbian operating system was a market leader, and their brand recognition was unmatched.

However, Nokia failed to anticipate the seismic shift towards smartphones. While they dabbled in touchscreen technology, they remained wedded to the Symbian platform, which lacked the user-friendliness and app ecosystem of the emerging iOS and Android operating systems. This allegiance to the status quo proved fatal.

Enter Samsung: The Challenger with a Vision

Samsung, on the other hand, embraced the smartphone revolution with open arms. They recognized the importance of a user-friendly interface and a robust app ecosystem. Samsung heavily invested in developing powerful Android-based smartphones with sleek designs and innovative features. They prioritized user experience and aggressively marketed their devices, capturing a significant portion of the market share.

The Innovation Paradox:

The story of Nokia and Samsung highlights a crucial paradox of innovation – successful companies often struggle to innovate from a position of strength. The very processes and structures that propelled them to the top can become barriers to change. Leaders become entrenched in their existing ideologies, and the "cult of the status quo" takes root.

Symptoms of the Status Quo:

Here are some tell-tale signs that a company may be suffering from an over-reliance on the status quo:

- **Aversion to risk-taking:** A culture that prioritizes short-term gains and avoids taking calculated risks on new ideas.
- **Silos and Bureaucracy:** Rigid departmental structures and bureaucratic processes that impede communication and collaboration.
- **Dismissive of new ideas:** A tendency to dismiss disruptive technologies or business models without thorough consideration.

- **Focus on internal metrics over customer needs:** Prioritization of internal performance indicators over understanding and exceeding customer expectations.

These symptoms can create a stagnant environment devoid of creativity and a breeding ground for complacency. In the next chapter, we'll explore the fear of failure – another powerful force that can contribute to the "cult of the status quo" and hinder a company's ability to innovate.

Chapter 3: Fear of Failure and the Innovation Paradox: How Risk Aversion Stifles Creativity and Innovation

The human psyche is wired for survival. Built-in aversion to risk has served us well throughout history, keeping us safe from danger. However, in the dynamic world of business, this very instinct can become a formidable foe of innovation. This chapter delves into the concept of the **Innovation Paradox** – how the fear of failure, a natural human response, can stifle creativity and ultimately hinder a company's ability to innovate and adapt.

The Innovation Paradox Explained

Imagine a company at a crossroads. One path leads towards safe, incremental improvements – tweaking existing products and processes. The other path leads towards the unknown – a bold new idea, a disruptive technology, a risky venture. The fear of failure looms large on this path. What if the new idea flops? What if the investment backfires? This fear can be a powerful deterrent, causing companies to shy away from innovation and cling to the familiar, even when the familiar is no longer the path to success.

Case Studies: New Blood Disrupts Old Guard

History is replete with examples of established companies brought to their knees by a new player, a challenger willing to embrace risk and disrupt the status quo. Let's explore five such stories:

1. Netflix vs. Blockbuster: Blockbuster, once the undisputed king of video rentals, reigned supreme with its vast brick-and-mortar network and convenient late-night rentals. However, they failed to anticipate the rise of online streaming, dismissing Netflix as a niche competitor. Blockbuster's fear of cannibalizing their core business with a new model (online rentals) coupled with a lack of investment in digital infrastructure ultimately led to their downfall. Netflix, on the other hand, embraced the online streaming revolution, offering a convenient and cost-effective way to watch movies. They weren't afraid to disrupt their own business model, and their willingness to take risks paid off handsomely.

2. Uber vs. Taxi Industry: The traditional taxi industry, characterized by slow response times, unpredictable pricing, and limited availability, was ripe for disruption. Enter Uber, a revolutionary ridesharing app that connected passengers with drivers through their smartphones. Uber's founders weren't afraid to challenge the status quo and battle entrenched regulations. They embraced innovation and risk, offering a more convenient and transparent experience for both riders and drivers. Traditional taxi companies, clinging to their outdated model and fearful of regulatory hurdles, were left behind in the dust.

3. Airbnb vs. Hospitality Industry: The hospitality industry, dominated by established hotel chains, offered a limited range of accommodation options with standardized experiences. Airbnb, a platform that allowed individuals to rent out their spare rooms or entire homes, emerged as a game-changer. Airbnb wasn't afraid to disrupt the traditional hospitality model, offering unique and often more affordable accommodation options. The established hotel chains, fearful of losing market share and hesitant to embrace a peer-to-peer rental model, were slow to react. Airbnb's willingness to take risks and challenge the status quo has transformed the travel industry.

4. Tesla vs. Traditional Automakers: The automotive industry, dominated by established car manufacturers, was slow to embrace electric vehicles (EVs). Tesla, under the visionary leadership of Elon Musk, emerged as a pioneer in the EV space. Tesla was not afraid to take risks, investing heavily in battery technology, autonomous driving features, and a sleek car design. Traditional automakers, fearful of the high upfront costs associated with EV development and hesitant to cannibalize their existing gasoline-powered vehicle sales, were slow to enter the EV market. Tesla's audacity and risk-taking have disrupted the auto industry, paving the way for a more sustainable future of transportation.

5. Dollar Shave Club vs. Razor Giants: The shaving industry, dominated by established giants like Gillette, offered a limited range of razors at premium prices. Dollar Shave Club, a subscription service that delivered high-quality razors directly to consumers at a fraction of the cost, emerged as a disruptive force. Dollar Shave Club wasn't afraid to challenge the status quo with their humorous marketing campaign and convenient subscription model. The established razor companies, fearful of losing market share and hesitant to deviate from their traditional retail model, were slow to respond. Dollar Shave Club's willingness to take risks and innovate has shaken up the shaving industry, offering consumers a more affordable and convenient option.

The High Cost of Risk Aversion

These case studies illustrate the high cost of risk aversion. Companies that cling to the status quo and shy away from bold ideas can find themselves blindsided by disruptive innovation. The fear of failure can paralyze decision-making, hindering the ability to adapt and evolve in a rapidly changing marketplace.

Creating a Culture of Calculated Risk-Taking

Fear of failure is a natural human emotion, but it doesn't have to be a crippling force. Companies can cultivate a culture that embraces calculated risk-taking, where innovation is encouraged and experimentation is valued. Here are some strategies to foster this environment:

- **Normalize Failure:** Shift the perception of failure from a stigma to a learning opportunity. Encourage employees to experiment, even if it means encountering setbacks. Focus on learning from mistakes and using those lessons to improve future endeavors.
- **Celebrate Small Wins:** Recognize and reward not just groundbreaking successes, but also small wins and incremental improvements that pave the way for future innovation.

- **Empower Employees:** Give employees the autonomy and resources to explore new ideas. Break down silos between departments and encourage cross-functional collaboration to foster diverse perspectives.
- **Implement a "Safe Space" for Ideas:** Create a designated space, physical or virtual, where employees feel comfortable sharing unconventional ideas without fear of ridicule or rejection.
- **Embrace Rapid Prototyping:** Encourage the creation of quick and inexpensive prototypes to test new concepts and gather user feedback early and often. This "fail fast, learn fast" approach minimizes wasted resources and allows for course correction before significant investments are made.
- **Invest in Innovation Training:** Provide employees with the skills and knowledge to develop and evaluate new ideas. This could include training in design thinking, user research, and business model innovation.
- **Reward Calculated Risks:** Recognize and reward employees who are willing to take calculated risks in pursuit of innovation. This incentivizes employees to step outside their comfort zones and embrace new challenges.
- **Lead by Example:** Leaders need to be vocal champions of innovation. They should demonstrate a willingness to take

risks and embrace change. This sets the tone for the entire organization and encourages employees to follow suit.

The Art of Calculated Risks

It's important to distinguish between recklessness and calculated risk-taking. Taking calculated risks involves careful analysis, thorough research, and a well-defined plan for mitigating potential downsides. Companies don't need to gamble everything on one untested idea. Instead, they can foster a culture of experimentation, where a series of smaller, calculated risks can lead to significant breakthroughs over time.

Conclusion: Embracing the Innovation Imperative

The fear of failure is a powerful force, but it doesn't have to be a barrier to innovation. By creating a culture of calculated risk-taking, fostering a safe space for ideas, and empowering employees, companies can overcome the innovation paradox. In today's dynamic business landscape, the ability to innovate is no longer a luxury; it's an imperative.

The next chapter will delve into the concept of "Cultivating a Culture of Innovation," exploring specific strategies and practices that companies can implement to create a fertile ground for new ideas and breakthrough thinking.

Chapter 4: Silencing Dissent: The Peril of Groupthink in Decision-Making

Imagine a boardroom filled with nodding heads, a chorus of agreement echoing through the air. New ideas are met with polite indifference, and dissenting voices remain silent. This scene, while seemingly harmonious, represents a dangerous phenomenon known as **groupthink**. Defined as the tendency for groups to prioritize conformity over critical thinking, groupthink can lead to flawed decision-making and hinder a company's ability to innovate. This chapter explores the perils of groupthink and underscores the importance of fostering diverse perspectives and challenging assumptions in the decision-making process.

The Seductive Siren Song of Conformity

Groupthink thrives in environments where harmony and consensus are valued above all else. Meetings become echo chambers, where dominant voices hold sway and dissenting opinions are discouraged. This pressure to conform stems from a desire to maintain group cohesion and avoid conflict. Employees may fear being ostracized or labeled as troublemakers if they voice concerns or challenge the prevailing group opinion.

The Innovation Killers: Symptoms of Groupthink

Several symptoms can indicate the presence of groupthink within a company:

- **An illusion of invulnerability:** The group develops an unyielding belief in its own correctness, leading to a dismissal of alternative viewpoints and a resistance to feedback.
- **Collective rationalization:** Members of the group downplay or ignore any warnings or potential risks associated with the proposed course of action.
- **Pressure to conform:** There exists an unspoken pressure to agree with the majority opinion, even if individuals harbor doubts or concerns.
- **Mind guards:** Certain individuals within the group unconsciously protect the leader from dissenting opinions, filtering out any information that contradicts the group's preferred course of action.
- **Direct stereotypes:** Negative stereotypes are applied to those who hold opposing views, further marginalizing dissenting voices.

These symptoms can create a myopic environment where critical thinking is stifled, and innovative solutions are overlooked. The following case study serves as a stark reminder of the dangers of groupthink.

The Bay of Pigs Fiasco: A Cautionary Tale

The Bay of Pigs invasion of 1961 stands as a chilling example of how groupthink can lead to disastrous consequences. The CIA, under immense pressure from President John F. Kennedy, planned a covert operation to overthrow the Cuban government led by Fidel Castro. Despite significant doubts expressed by intelligence analysts about the feasibility of the plan, a culture of groupthink prevailed. Surrounded by advisors who echoed his own views, Kennedy approved the invasion, which ultimately resulted in a humiliating defeat for the United States.

The Power of Dissent: Championing Diverse Perspectives

It's crucial to recognize that dissent is not a sign of disloyalty; it's a safeguard against flawed decision-making. Companies that foster an environment where diverse perspectives are valued and healthy debate is encouraged are more likely to arrive at innovative solutions. Here are some strategies to cultivate such an environment:

- **Assemble Diverse Teams:** Build teams with individuals from different backgrounds, experiences, and skillsets. This diversity of thought can spark creative solutions and challenge established assumptions.
- **Encourage Healthy Debate:** Create a safe space for open dialogue and constructive criticism. Leaders should actively solicit diverse viewpoints and avoid shutting down dissenting voices.
- **Appoint a Devil's Advocate:** Assign someone the role of devil's advocate, whose responsibility is to challenge assumptions, identify potential flaws in the plan, and present alternative perspectives.
- **Embrace Psychological Safety:** Cultivate a company culture where employees feel safe to speak their minds without fear of retribution. This psychological safety is essential for fostering honest and open communication.
- **Reward Dissent (the Right Way):** Recognize and reward employees who are willing to voice concerns or present alternative viewpoints, as long as their dissent is based on facts and constructive criticism.

Conclusion: Innovation Through Inclusive Decision-Making

By mitigating the risks of groupthink and fostering an environment that embraces diverse perspectives, companies can harness the power of dissent to drive innovation. The ability to challenge assumptions, consider alternative viewpoints, and engage in healthy debate is essential for making sound decisions and navigating the ever-changing business landscape.

Chapter 5: Cultivating a Culture of Innovation: Sparking Creativity and Embracing the New

The ability to innovate is no longer a luxury; it's the lifeblood of any company striving for long-term success. In today's dynamic marketplace, companies that cling to the status quo and fail to embrace new ideas risk getting left behind. This chapter explores the concept of a **culture of innovation** and outlines specific strategies that companies can implement to foster creativity, break down silos, and empower employees to become active participants in the innovation process.

Building a Fertile Ground for New Ideas

A culture of innovation is not something that can be mandated; it needs to be nurtured and cultivated. It's an environment where creativity is encouraged, experimentation is valued, and new ideas are met with open minds and a willingness to explore their potential. Here are some key strategies to cultivate such a culture:

1. Foster a Growth Mindset: Shift the company mindset from one that values perfectionism and risk aversion to one that embraces learning and growth. Encourage employees to see challenges as opportunities to learn and improve, and view failures as stepping stones on the path to success.

2. Encourage Curiosity and Exploration: Spark a sense of curiosity within your employees. Provide opportunities for them to learn new skills, explore emerging technologies, and attend industry conferences to stay abreast of the latest trends. Curiosity fuels creativity and opens doors to new possibilities.

3. Embrace Open Innovation: Don't limit innovation to internal resources. Embrace the concept of open innovation, where companies collaborate with external partners, startups, and universities to tap into a wider pool of knowledge and expertise. Open innovation can accelerate the ideation process and bring fresh perspectives to the table.

4. Break Down Silos and Encourage Collaboration: Innovation often thrives at the intersection of different disciplines. Break down the walls between departments and encourage cross-functional collaboration. Foster a team environment where knowledge is shared freely, and diverse perspectives are valued.

5. Reward and Recognize Innovation Efforts: Don't just pay lip service to innovation. Recognize and reward employees who contribute to the innovation process, whether through successful ideas or even well-executed failures that yielded valuable lessons. This incentivizes employees to keep innovating and taking risks.

6. Celebrate Experimentation and Prototyping: Encourage experimentation and rapid prototyping as a way to test new ideas and gather user feedback early and often. Building a "fail fast, learn fast" culture allows for course correction before significant investments are made.

7. Invest in Design Thinking: Design thinking is a human-centered approach to problem-solving that emphasizes empathy, user research, and iterative prototyping. By incorporating design thinking principles into the innovation process, companies can develop solutions that truly meet the needs of their customers.

8. Empower Employees: Give employees the autonomy and resources to develop and pursue their own ideas. This empowers employees to take ownership of the innovation process and become active participants in shaping the future of the company.

9. Lead by Example: Leaders play a crucial role in setting the tone for a culture of innovation. Leaders must be vocal champions of new ideas, demonstrate a willingness to take risks, and embrace change.

Beware the Revolving Door: Caution for Departing Employees

While fostering a culture of innovation is crucial, it's equally important to address the potential downside of an overly creative environment – employee turnover. Companies that invest heavily in cultivating a culture of innovation may find themselves unintentionally creating a breeding ground for restless minds who are constantly seeking the next big challenge. This can lead to a revolving door of talent, where employees leave after a few years to pursue new opportunities.

Here are some strategies to mitigate this risk:

- **Invest in Employee Development:** Provide opportunities for employees to learn new skills and grow their careers within the company. Offer training programs, mentorship opportunities, and challenging projects that keep employees engaged and motivated.
- **Promote Work-Life Balance:** Recognize that innovation thrives on a well-rested workforce. Promote healthy work-life balance by offering flexible work arrangements and encouraging employees to take breaks and disconnect from work outside of office hours.
- **Foster a Sense of Community:** Cultivate a strong company culture where employees feel valued and appreciated. Create

opportunities for social interaction and team building to foster a sense of belonging and camaraderie.

- **Offer Competitive Compensation and Benefits:** While innovation may be a driving force, it can't exist in a vacuum. Offer competitive compensation and benefits packages to retain top talent and incentivize them to stay and contribute their ideas to the company's continued success.

Conclusion: Innovation: A Continuous Journey

Cultivating a culture of innovation is not a one-time event; it's an ongoing process that requires continuous effort and commitment from leadership and employees.

Chapter 6: Embracing Disruption: Transforming Threats into Opportunities

Disruption. The very word evokes a sense of chaos and uncertainty. In the business world, disruption refers to the introduction of a game-changing technology, business model, or competitor that fundamentally alters the way an industry operates. While disruption can be a threat to established companies, it also presents a tremendous opportunity for those who can adapt and evolve. This chapter explores how companies can shift their perspective on disruption, viewing it not as a threat but as a catalyst for growth and innovation.

From Threat to Opportunity: Reframing Disruption

The fear of disruption can be paralyzing. Companies may cling to outdated models and resist change, ultimately succumbing to the forces of innovation. However, a more proactive approach exists.

Companies can choose to embrace disruption, viewing it as an opportunity to reinvent themselves and stay ahead of the curve. Here's why:

- **Disruption Creates New Markets:** Disruption often leads to the creation of entirely new markets. Companies that can identify these emerging markets and adapt their offerings accordingly can unlock significant growth opportunities.
- **Disruption Fuels Innovation:** The threat of disruption can be a powerful motivator for innovation. Companies facing disruption are forced to re-evaluate their existing models and explore new ways of doing business. This can lead to the development of groundbreaking products, services, and business models.
- **Disruption Levels the Playing Field:** Disruption can disrupt established hierarchies and create opportunities for new players to enter the market. This can be advantageous for companies that are agile and adaptable, allowing them to gain a competitive edge.

Learning from the Masters: Companies that Thrived on Disruption

History is replete with examples of companies that not only survived disruption but thrived on it. Here are five such stories:

1. Amazon vs. Brick-and-Mortar Retail: The rise of e-commerce, pioneered by Amazon, fundamentally altered the way people shop. Traditional brick-and-mortar retailers who failed to adapt to online shopping suffered significant losses. However, some retailers, like Walmart, embraced the online marketplace, investing in robust e-commerce platforms and omnichannel strategies that seamlessly blend online and offline shopping experiences.

1. Netflix vs. Blockbuster: Blockbuster, once the undisputed king of video rentals, failed to anticipate the rise of online streaming services like Netflix. Their overreliance on physical brick-and-mortar stores and a late entry into the streaming market ultimately led to their downfall. Netflix, on the other hand, embraced the shift towards online streaming, offering a vast library of content and a convenient subscription model, securing their position as a leader in the entertainment industry.

2. **Tesla vs. Traditional Automakers:** The traditional automotive industry has been slow to embrace electric vehicles (EVs). Tesla, under the visionary leadership of Elon Musk, emerged as a pioneer in the EV space, offering high-performance, stylish electric vehicles with innovative features like self-driving technology. Traditional automakers, fearful of the high upfront costs associated with EV development, are now playing catch-up, investing heavily in electrification to compete with Tesla.

These examples highlight how companies that embrace disruption and adapt to changing market dynamics can not only survive but thrive. The key lies in recognizing disruptive forces early on, understanding the opportunities they present, and having the agility to adapt and innovate.

The Disruption Mindset: Embracing Change and Experimentation

Cultivating a **disruption mindset** is crucial for any company that wants to thrive in today's dynamic business landscape. This mindset is characterized by the following:

- **Constant vigilance:** Actively scan the horizon for emerging trends and disruptive technologies that could impact your industry.
- **Openness to new ideas:** Embrace new ideas, even if they seem unconventional or challenge the status quo.
- **Willingness to experiment:** Be willing to experiment with new business models, technologies, and approaches.
- **A focus on customer needs:** Keep a laser focus on understanding and exceeding the evolving needs of your customers.

Chapter 7: Building Bridges Between Departments: Fostering Collaboration and Information Sharing

In today's complex business environment, success often hinges on the ability to break down silos and foster collaboration across different departments. Imagine a company where marketing operates in a vacuum, unaware of the latest product features being developed by engineering. Sales might struggle to close deals because they lack insights into customer support issues. This lack of communication and information sharing can lead to inefficiencies, missed opportunities, and ultimately, hinder a company's ability to innovate and compete effectively.

This chapter explores the importance of building bridges between departments and outlines strategies to encourage collaboration and information sharing across different functions within an organization.

The Perils of Silos: Why Collaboration Matters

Silos, or isolated departments with limited communication, can be a major obstacle to organizational success. Here's why collaboration is crucial:

- **Improved Decision-Making:** When different departments share information and expertise, companies can make more informed decisions that take into account all aspects of the business.

- **Enhanced Innovation:** Collaboration fosters cross-pollination of ideas, leading to the development of more creative and innovative solutions.
- **Increased Efficiency:** When departments work together seamlessly, processes become more streamlined, and redundancies are eliminated.
- **Improved Customer Experience:** Collaboration ensures a more unified customer experience, as different departments work together to meet customer needs.

Strategies for Building Bridges: From Walls to Collaboration

Here are some key strategies for breaking down silos and fostering collaboration across departments:

- **Cross-Functional Teams:** Create cross-functional teams that bring together individuals from different departments to work on specific projects. This exposes team members to diverse perspectives and encourages knowledge sharing.
- **Shared Goals and Metrics:** Establish shared goals and metrics that incentivize departments to work together towards the company's overall success. This fosters a sense of collective responsibility and discourages departmental competition.

- **Open Communication Channels:** Create open communication channels that facilitate the flow of information between departments. This could involve regular meetings, internal communication platforms, or even informal social events that encourage interaction.
- **Knowledge Sharing Initiatives:** Implement knowledge sharing initiatives such as brown bag lunches, internal knowledge repositories, or mentorship programs where employees from different departments can learn from each other's expertise.
- **Leadership Commitment:** Leaders play a crucial role in promoting collaboration. They need to model collaborative behavior, break down departmental biases, and champion cross-functional initiatives.
- **Technology Tools:** Leverage technology tools like project management platforms, communication platforms, and collaboration software to facilitate communication and information sharing across departments.

Building a Culture of Collaboration

Fostering collaboration is not just about setting up structures and processes; it's about cultivating a culture that values teamwork, open communication, and information sharing. Here's how to create such a culture:

- **Recognize and Reward Collaboration:** Recognize and reward employees who demonstrate collaborative behavior and actively contribute to cross-functional initiatives.
- **Promote Transparency:** Foster a culture of transparency where information is readily shared across departments. This builds trust and encourages open communication.
- **Celebrate Diversity:** Embrace the diversity of perspectives and experiences that different departments bring to the table. This diversity fuels creativity and innovation.
- **Focus on the "We" not the "Me":** Shift the company culture from one that prioritizes individual successes to one that emphasizes collective achievements. This fosters a sense of shared purpose and encourages collaboration.

Conclusion: The Power of Collaboration

In today's dynamic business landscape, companies that foster collaboration across departments are better positioned to innovate, adapt, and achieve sustainable success. By breaking down silos, encouraging information sharing, and cultivating a culture of teamwork, companies can unlock the collective potential of their workforce and become more competitive in the ever-evolving marketplace.

Chapter 8: The Power of Customer Insights: How Understanding Your Customers Drives Innovation

Customers are the lifeblood of any business. Their needs, wants, and frustrations hold the key to unlocking innovation and developing products and services that truly resonate. This chapter delves into the power of customer insights and explores how companies can leverage this knowledge to drive innovation and achieve sustainable success.

Beyond Transactions: Unearthing the Customer's Voice

Many companies make the mistake of viewing customers solely as a source of revenue. However, to truly thrive, companies need to go beyond transactions and develop a deep understanding of their customers' needs, motivations, and pain points. Here's why customer insights are crucial:

- **Identifying New Opportunities:** Customer insights can reveal unmet needs and emerging trends, allowing companies to identify new opportunities for innovation and product development.

- **Developing Customer-Centric Solutions:** By understanding customer needs, companies can design and develop products and services that directly address their customers' problems and provide true value.
- **Building Customer Loyalty:** When companies demonstrate that they understand and care about their customers' needs, it fosters loyalty and trust, leading to repeat business and positive word-of-mouth marketing.
- **Improving Customer Experience:** Customer insights can guide the development of a more seamless and customer-centric experience across all touchpoints.

Case Studies: Innovation Driven by Customer Insights

Here are four compelling examples of how companies leveraged customer insights to drive innovation:

1. Intuit: Understanding the Small Business Owner's Pain Points

Intuit, the maker of popular financial software like QuickBooks, didn't achieve success by simply offering accounting software. They took the time to understand the challenges faced by small business owners, including managing finances, tracking expenses, and filing taxes. By listening to their customers, Intuit developed user-friendly software that streamlined these processes and addressed the specific needs of small businesses.

2. Nike: Innovation Inspired by Athletes

Nike, the global sportswear giant, doesn't rely solely on designers to come up with new and innovative products. They actively engage with athletes at all levels, from elite professionals to weekend warriors. By understanding their needs and the challenges they face during training and competition, Nike develops performance-enhancing apparel and footwear that pushes the boundaries of athletic innovation.

3. LEGO: Co-Creation with the Customer

LEGO, the iconic building block toy company, understands the power of customer engagement. They've developed platforms like LEGO Ideas, where users can submit their own creative building ideas and vote for their favorites. LEGO then considers these user-generated ideas for future product development, fostering a sense of community and ownership among their customers.

4. Netflix: Tailoring Content to User Preferences

Netflix revolutionized the way we watch movies and television shows. A key ingredient to their success is their sophisticated recommendation engine, which leverages customer data to curate personalized content suggestions for each user. By understanding their customers' viewing habits and preferences, Netflix delivers a more engaging and satisfying entertainment experience.

Unearthing Customer Insights: A Toolkit for Innovation

Companies can leverage various tools and strategies to gather valuable customer insights:

- **Customer Surveys and Feedback Forms:** Collect direct feedback from customers through surveys and feedback forms to understand their opinions, needs, and pain points.
- **Customer Interviews:** Conduct in-depth interviews with customers to gain a deeper understanding of their motivations, behaviors, and challenges.
- **Customer Support Analysis:** Analyze customer support interactions to identify recurring issues and areas for improvement.

- **Social Media Listening:** Monitor social media conversations to see what customers are saying about your brand, products, and competitors.
- **User Testing and Usability Studies:** Observe how customers interact with your products and services to identify areas for improvement.

Conclusion: The Customer-Centric Imperative

In today's competitive business landscape, understanding your customers is no longer a luxury; it's a necessity. By prioritizing customer insights and leveraging these insights to drive innovation, companies can develop products and services that truly resonate with their target audience, build stronger customer relationships, and achieve sustainable success.

Chapter 10: Future-Focused Thinking: Developing Strategies to Scan the Horizon for Emerging Trends

In today's rapidly evolving business landscape, the ability to anticipate and adapt to change is paramount. Companies that bury their heads in the sand and fail to consider future trends risk getting blindsided by disruption. This chapter explores the concept of **future-focused thinking** and outlines strategies for companies to scan the horizon for emerging trends that could impact their industry and inform their long-term success.

Why Future-Proofing Matters: The Power of Foresight

Future-focused thinking is not about predicting the future with absolute certainty. It's about developing a strategic awareness of potential disruptions, emerging technologies, and shifting societal values that could impact your business. Here's why this foresight is crucial:

- **Early Warning System:** Identifying emerging trends early on allows companies to prepare for potential disruptions, develop contingency plans, and adjust their strategies accordingly.
- **Innovation Inspiration:** Understanding future trends can spark innovation, leading to the development of new

products, services, and business models that capitalize on emerging opportunities.
- **Competitive Advantage:** Companies that embrace future-focused thinking gain a competitive edge by being better prepared to adapt to change and meet the evolving needs of their customers.

Building Your Futurescape: Tools and Techniques for Trendspotting

There's no one-size-fits-all approach to future-focused thinking. Here's a toolkit of strategies companies can employ to scan the horizon for emerging trends:

- **Weak Signal Detection:** Train your team to identify weak signals, which are seemingly insignificant pieces of information that may hint at larger trends to come. This could involve monitoring social media conversations, industry publications, and academic research.
- **Scenario Planning:** Develop different scenarios for the future, considering various possibilities and potential disruptions. This exercise helps companies brainstorm potential challenges and opportunities associated with each scenario.
- **Competitive Intelligence:** Keep a close eye on your competitors and what they're doing. Are they investing in new

technologies? Partnering with disruptive startups? Understanding their moves can shed light on future trends in your industry.

- **Trend Reports and Industry Analysis:** Leverage the insights of industry experts and research firms that publish reports on emerging trends and future forecasts.
- **Emerging Technology Exploration:** Stay abreast of advancements in artificial intelligence, robotics, biotechnology, and other emerging technologies that could reshape your industry.
- **Customer Insights:** Don't just focus on external trends; pay attention to your customers' evolving needs and preferences. What are their pain points? What unmet needs can you address with future-oriented solutions?

From Insights to Action: Turning Trends into Tangible Strategies

Spotting trends is just the first step. The key lies in translating those insights into actionable strategies:

- **Strategic Planning:** Integrate future-focused thinking into your strategic planning process. Consider how emerging trends might impact your long-term goals and objectives.
- **Innovation Pipeline Development:** Use trend insights to fuel your innovation pipeline, identifying opportunities for new product development, service offerings, and business model innovation.
- **Capability Building:** Invest in developing the capabilities and skillsets needed to thrive in the future. This could involve training your workforce on new technologies or fostering a culture of experimentation.
- **Scenario Testing:** Test your strategies against different future scenarios to ensure your company is prepared for a range of possibilities.

Case Study:

LEGO (Denmark): A leading toy company that has embraced innovation by staying true to its core product while expanding offerings and fostering a creative community.

Spotify (Sweden): A music streaming giant that pioneered a freemium model and personalized music recommendations, disrupting the traditional music industry.

Dassault Systèmes (France): A 3DEXPERIENCE company that provides 3D design, simulation, and data management software, at the forefront of technological innovation.

ARM Holdings (UK): A designer of semiconductor intellectual property (IP) cores and related processor technologies, widely used in mobile device.

: Building a Culture of Foresight

Future-focused thinking is not a one-time exercise; it needs to become ingrained in a company's culture. Here are some ways to cultivate a culture of foresight:

- **Leadership Commitment:** Leaders need to champion future-focused thinking and set the tone for the organization.
- **Cross-Functional Collaboration:** Encourage collaboration between different departments to ensure diverse perspectives are considered when analyzing future trends.

- **A Learning Mindset:** Foster a culture of continuous learning and encourage employees to stay curious about the future.
- **Rewarding Trendspotting:** Recognize and reward employees who identify and bring to light potential future trends.

Conclusion: Charting Your Course to the Future

In today's dynamic business environment, companies that embrace future-focused thinking are better equipped to navigate uncertainty, capitalize on emerging opportunities, and secure their long-term success. By developing a systematic approach to scanning the horizon, translating trends into actionable strategies, and fostering a culture of foresight.

Chapter 11: Building an Innovation Engine: The Powerhouse of New Ideas

In today's fiercely competitive business landscape, the ability to generate and commercialize groundbreaking ideas is no longer a luxury; it's an imperative for sustainable success. This chapter delves into the concept of an **innovation engine**, a systematic framework for identifying, nurturing, and testing new ideas that have the potential to transform your business. We'll explore the key components of a successful innovation engine and provide practical steps for companies of all sizes to build their own powerhouse of creativity.

Beyond Brainstorming: The Systematic Approach to Innovation

Many companies struggle with innovation because they rely on sporadic brainstorming sessions or individual heroics. An innovation engine, however, takes a more structured and systematic approach. It provides a defined process for capturing ideas, evaluating their potential, and developing them into viable products or services.

The Essential Building Blocks of an Innovation Engine

A robust innovation engine is comprised of several key elements:

1. A Culture of Openness and Creativity:

- **Psychological Safety:** Foster an environment where employees feel safe to share ideas, even if they seem unconventional or risky. Encourage constructive criticism and open communication.
- **Diversity of Thought:** Assemble a team with diverse backgrounds, experiences, and perspectives to spark creative collisions and generate a wider range of ideas.
- **Rewarding Curiosity:** Encourage employees to be curious and explore new possibilities. Recognize and reward employees

who demonstrate a questioning attitude and a willingness to challenge the status quo.

2. Idea Capture and Management System:

- **Multiple Idea Submission Channels:** Provide multiple avenues for employees to submit ideas, including online platforms, suggestion boxes, or internal innovation challenges.
- **Idea Filtering and Prioritization:** Establish a clear process for filtering and prioritizing ideas based on their feasibility, potential impact, and alignment with company strategy.
- **Idea Tracking and Management Software:** Utilize software or online platforms to track the progress of ideas, facilitate collaboration, and ensure no good idea gets lost in the shuffle.

3. The Power of Experimentation and Rapid Prototyping:

- **Embrace Failure as Learning:** Shift the company culture away from a fear of failure and towards viewing it as a valuable learning opportunity. Encourage experimentation and rapid prototyping to test ideas quickly and cheaply.
- **Minimum Viable Products (MVPs):** Develop minimum viable products (MVPs) – basic versions of a product or service – to test core assumptions and gather user feedback early in the development process.

- **A/B Testing:** Leverage A/B testing to compare different versions of ideas and features, gaining data-driven insights on what resonates most with your target audience.

4. **Dedicated Resources and Investment:**

    - **Innovation Team or Department:** Consider establishing a dedicated innovation team or department responsible for overseeing the entire innovation process, from idea capture to implementation.
    - **Innovation Budget:** Allocate a specific budget for innovation initiatives, including funding for prototyping, user research, and piloting new ideas.
    - **Training and Development:** Provide training and development opportunities for employees to enhance their creative problem-solving skills and design thinking capabilities.

5. **Metrics and Measurement:**

    - **Defining Innovation Success:** Clearly define what innovation success means for your company. Is it focused on revenue generation, cost reduction, or customer satisfaction? Having clear metrics allows you to track progress and measure the impact of your innovation efforts.

- **Idea Stage-Specific Metrics:** Develop metrics relevant to different stages of the innovation process. For example, track the number of ideas submitted, rate of successful prototypes, and time to market for new products or services.

Putting the Engine into Action: A Step-by-Step Guide

Here's a practical roadmap for companies to build their own innovation engine:

Step 1: Assess Your Innovation Maturity

Begin by evaluating your company's current innovation capabilities. Are you an idea generation powerhouse, or do you struggle to move ideas beyond the brainstorming stage? Identifying your strengths and weaknesses will help you prioritize areas for improvement.

Step 2: Define Your Innovation Goals

What do you hope to achieve through your innovation efforts? Do you want to develop disruptive new products, improve existing ones, or become more efficient in your operations? Clearly defined goals will guide your innovation strategy and resource allocation.

Step 3: Assemble Your Innovation Team

Identify and empower a team of individuals with diverse backgrounds, skills, and a passion for innovation. This team can be responsible for overseeing the engine, managing incoming ideas, and guiding them through the development process.

Step 4: Establish Idea Capture Channels

Create multiple avenues for employees to submit ideas, including online platforms, suggestion boxes, or innovation challenges with specific themes. Make sure the submission process.

is easy, accessible, and encourages anonymity if desired.

Step 5: Develop an Idea Filtering and Prioritization System

Establish clear criteria for filtering and prioritizing ideas. This might involve considering factors like:

- **Alignment with Company Strategy:** Does the idea support your overall business goals and objectives?
- **Market Need:** Does the idea address a genuine need or pain point for your target customer?
- **Feasibility:** Is the idea technically and commercially feasible given your current resources and capabilities?
- **Potential Impact:** What is the potential upside of the idea in terms of revenue growth, cost savings, or customer satisfaction?

Step 6: Embrace Experimentation and Rapid Prototyping

Move beyond theoretical discussions and encourage experimentation. Develop MVPs to test core assumptions and gather user feedback early on. Utilize rapid prototyping techniques that allow you to create functional models quickly and iterate based on user insights.

Step 7: Invest in the Right Tools and Technology

Consider implementing innovation management software to streamline the idea submission, tracking, and collaboration process. Explore online platforms that facilitate A/B testing and user research to gather valuable data on new ideas.

Step 8: Celebrate Innovation and Share Success Stories

Recognize and celebrate employees who actively participate in the innovation process. Share success stories of how new ideas have benefited the company, motivating others to contribute and fostering a culture of innovation.

From Idea to Impact: The Innovation Journey

Building an innovation engine is not a one-time event; it's an ongoing process. Here's how ideas typically navigate the innovation engine:

- **Idea Submission:** Employees submit ideas through various channels, providing a clear description, potential benefits, and any supporting documentation.
- **Idea Screening:** The innovation team or a designated committee screens ideas based on the established criteria, filtering out less promising concepts.
- **Idea Development:** Promising ideas are assigned to a small team for further development. This team might conduct market research, develop prototypes, and refine the concept.
- **Idea Testing:** Prototypes are tested with target users to gather feedback and assess potential market fit. A/B testing might be employed to compare different iterations of the idea.
- **Idea Go/No-Go Decision:** Based on test results and feedback, a decision is made to move forward with the idea, shelve it, or iterate further based on learnings.
- **Implementation and Launch:** For approved ideas, a dedicated team oversees the development, launch, and marketing of the new product or service.

Continuous Improvement: Fueling the Innovation Engine

A successful innovation engine requires constant monitoring and adaptation. Here are some ways to keep your engine running smoothly:

- **Gather Feedback from Stakeholders:** Regularly solicit feedback from employees, customers, and other stakeholders on the effectiveness of your innovation process. Use this feedback to identify areas for improvement.
- **Benchmarking and Learning from Others:** Study the innovation practices of successful companies in your industry and beyond. Identify best practices and adapt them to your own context.
- **Embrace Open Innovation:** Consider partnering with external startups, universities, or research institutions to access new ideas and expertise.
- **Leadership Commitment:** Leaders play a crucial role in championing innovation and creating an environment that fosters creativity and risk-taking.

Building a Culture of Innovation: The Engine for Long-Term Success

In today's rapidly evolving business landscape, companies that prioritize innovation are better positioned to thrive. By building a robust innovation engine, companies can cultivate a culture of creativity, systematically generate groundbreaking ideas, and transform those ideas into products and services that drive growth and success. Remember, innovation is not a magic bullet; it's a continuous process that requires dedication, a commitment to experimentation, and a willingness to embrace change. By following the steps outlined in this chapter and fostering a culture that celebrates new ideas, companies can build an innovation engine that fuels their long-term success.

Chapter 12: Leading for Innovation: The Role of Leadership in Fostering a Culture of Change

In today's dynamic business environment, innovation is no longer a luxury; it's an imperative for survival. But fostering a truly innovative culture requires more than just encouraging employees to "think outside the box." It demands visionary leadership that creates a supportive environment where creativity flourishes, calculated risks are embraced, and change is seen as an opportunity, not a threat. This chapter explores the critical role leaders play in igniting the flame of innovation and guiding their teams towards a future fueled by groundbreaking ideas.

Beyond the Status Quo: The Qualities of an Innovative Leader

Innovative leaders aren't content with maintaining the status quo. They possess a unique set of qualities that empower them to champion change and drive their organizations forward. Here are some key characteristics that define an innovative leader:

- **Visionary Mindset:** They have a clear vision for the future of the company and can articulate a compelling story about what the organization can achieve through innovation.
- **Strategic Foresight:** They are adept at scanning the horizon for emerging trends and understanding how these trends might impact their industry.
- **Customer Obsession:** They are laser-focused on understanding their customers' needs and exceeding their expectations. They view innovation as a tool to address customer pain points and create new value propositions.
- **Risk Tolerance:** They understand that innovation often involves taking calculated risks. They create a safe space for experimentation and encourage employees to learn from failures.
- **Empowerment and Collaboration:** They empower their teams to take ownership of ideas, make decisions, and collaborate effectively across departments.
- **Communication and Storytelling:** They are skilled communicators who can articulate the vision for innovation and inspire employees to contribute their best efforts.
- **Adaptability and Agility:** They recognize that the business landscape is constantly evolving and foster a culture of adaptability and agility to navigate change effectively.

Building an Innovation-Friendly Culture: Leader-Driven Strategies

Leaders play a crucial role in shaping the company culture and setting the stage for innovation to flourish. Here are some strategies leaders can employ to cultivate an innovation-friendly environment:

- **Clearly Define Innovation Goals:** Clearly articulate what innovation means for your company. Is it about developing disruptive new products, improving efficiency, or fostering a culture of continuous improvement? Defining these goals provides a roadmap for your innovation efforts.
- **Celebrate Curiosity and Experimentation:** Encourage employees to ask questions, explore new possibilities, and experiment with different approaches. Normalize failure as a learning opportunity and celebrate successful experiments, regardless of the outcome.
- **Provide Resources and Support:** Allocate necessary resources for innovation initiatives, including funding for prototyping, training in creative problem-solving techniques, and access to relevant tools and technologies.
- **Break Down Silos and Encourage Collaboration:** Foster cross-functional collaboration by breaking down departmental silos and encouraging teams to work together

on innovation projects. Diversity of thought is critical for generating new ideas.

- **Recognize and Reward Innovation Champions:** Acknowledge and reward employees who actively participate in the innovation process, generate valuable ideas, or champion new approaches. This reinforces the desired behaviors and motivates others to contribute.
- **Lead by Example:** Leaders need to walk the talk. Be willing to experiment yourself, take calculated risks, and demonstrate a commitment to innovation through your actions.
- **Open Communication and Transparency:** Foster a culture of open communication and transparency. Encourage employees to share ideas and concerns freely, without fear of retribution. This creates a safe space for creativity.

From Vision to Reality: The Power of Innovative Leadership

Leaders who embrace innovation and create an environment that empowers their teams are the driving force behind groundbreaking ideas and transformative change. They understand that innovation is not a solo endeavor; it's a collaborative effort fueled by a shared vision, a spirit of experimentation, and a willingness to embrace change. By cultivating an innovation-friendly culture and leading by example, leaders can unlock the collective creativity of their workforce and propel their organizations towards a future fueled by groundbreaking ideas.

Remember, innovation is not a destination; it's a continuous journey. Leaders who champion innovation and foster a culture of change ensure their companies are well-equipped to navigate the ever-evolving business landscape and achieve sustainable success.

Conclusion:

The journey through this book has explored the exhilarating world of innovation. We've delved into the strategies of companies renowned for their groundbreaking ideas, unveiled the tools and techniques for future-focused thinking, and examined the leadership principles that cultivate a culture of creativity and change.

At its core, this book is a call to action. Innovation is not the exclusive domain of Silicon Valley giants or tech startups. It's a mindset, a strategic approach, and a continuous process that any company, regardless of size or industry, can embrace. By fostering a culture of curiosity, experimentation, and openness to new ideas, companies can unlock their true innovative potential.

The Key Ingredients for Your Innovation Recipe

As you embark on your own innovation journey, here are some key takeaways to keep in mind:

- **Customer Focus:** Never lose sight of your customers. Innovation should be driven by a deep understanding of their needs and a relentless pursuit of exceeding their expectations.
- **Embrace the Future:** Develop a strategic foresight capability to identify emerging trends and disruptive technologies that could impact your industry.
- **Build an Innovation Engine:** Establish a systematic process for capturing ideas, evaluating their potential, and developing them into viable products or services.
- **Empower Your People:** Cultivate a culture of creativity and collaboration. Empower your employees to take ownership of ideas, experiment, and learn from failures.
- **Lead by Example:** Leaders play a critical role in setting the tone for innovation. Champion change, embrace calculated risks, and demonstrate a commitment to innovation through your actions.

Innovation is a Continuous Journey

Remember, innovation is not a one-time event; it's a continuous journey. There will be setbacks, unexpected challenges, and moments of doubt. But by fostering a culture of innovation and perseverance, you can ensure your company is well-equipped to navigate change, seize opportunities, and achieve long-term success.

The future belongs to those who believe in the beauty of their dreams. – Eleanor Roosevelt

May this book serve as a springboard for your own innovation journey. Embrace the challenge, unleash your creativity, and embark on a path of continuous improvement, fueled by groundbreaking ideas and a commitment to shaping a brighter future.

Thanks for your time.

www.ingramcontent.com/pod-product-compliance
Lightning Source LLC
Chambersburg PA
CBHW082217220526
45470CB00010B/3204